ASHIWAZA II

JUDO MASTERCLASS TECHNIQUES

Ashiwaza II

Ouchi–Gari   *Kouchi–Gari*

Kosoto–Gari   *Hiza–Guruma*

Michael Swain
with
Oon Oon Yeoh

Photographs by David Finch

Ippon Books

First published by
Ippon Books Ltd.
55 Long Lane
London N3 2HY

British Library Cataloguing in Publication Data

Swain, Michael and Oon Oon Yeoh
    Ashiwaza II: Judo Masterclass Techniques
    1. Judo
    2. Title

ISBN 1 874572 65 8

ACKNOWLEDGEMENTS
Ali Moghadas, my student at San Jose State University, undertook the arduous task of being *uke* for the entire photo session.

David Finch of Judo Photos Unlimited took time off his busy schedule to photograph the demonstration sequences and provided great competition shots from his extensive judo library.

Ulrich Klocke and Ed Ferrie provided additional photographs.

Tony Sweeney, long-time coach at The Budokwai, London, contributed to the history section of this book.

Oon Oon Yeoh, of Malaysia, co-wrote this book and oversaw production from conception to completion.

Nicolas Soames edited this book and compiled the index.

Artwork, design and layout by Ben Moss, of Austin, Texas.

To all the individuals above and others who helped make this project a success, I thank you.

Printed in Great Britain by Redwood Books.

Contents

Foreword

Michael Swain's victory in the -71kg category of the 1987 World Championships in Essen, Germany, was a popular one, as everyone who was there to see it will attest. He had done it the hard way—beating Toshihiko Koga, the Japanese favourite (later World and Olympic champion) and, in the final, Marc Alexandre of France (later Olympic champion). He was the first American male to win a world title.

What was equally significant was that Swain won with style. His judo has always been characterized by a very upright stance, fluid and precise movements, and bold attacking gestures. He had been to Japan as a teenager, survived the initiation, and emerged a fighter capable of taking on all styles—from classical to mauler—without compromising his own judo. This can be seen clearly in the demonstrations in *Ashiwaza II*.

While he was known for a number of techniques—notably *tai-otoshi*—it was no coincidence that he threw Koga with *ouchi-gari*. This technique, as he explains, was one that served him well when trying to survive as a youngster in the toughest *dojos* in Japan.

In his contribution to the *Masterclass Techniques* series, Michael Swain presents his understanding of the technique as well as other related *ashiwaza*. This, he is eminently suited to do. He comments in his text that *ashiwaza* formed the basis of most of his attacks. Everyone who has done *randori* with him, as I have, will remember the slightly unnerving experience of this elusive shape moving in front of you, difficult to pin down, tapping at a leg here or a leg there, and then suddenly attacking with an *ouchi-gari* that was horrifyingly crisp and decisive!

This is judo to be studied. Very few practising *judoka* work without one of the four techniques covered in this volume. Drawing on Swain's experience at the very top level will no doubt pay considerable dividends.

Nicolas Soames
Masterclass Series Editor

My greatest rival.

Here I am coming to grips with the Olympic and World lightweight
champion Toshihiko Koga, in the third round of the 1987 Essen
World Championships. I knew I had my work cut out for me—but I
prevailed, thanks to my favourite *ashiwaza, ouchi-gari.*

My favourite judoka.

A picture of me with my wife, Chie Ishii, the Brazilian
ashiwaza specialist who swept me off my feet!

Ashiwaza: A Personal View

I was eight years old when I began judo. My uncle had practised judo when he was in the military. At the time, judo was quite popular among military men in the States. He encouraged my brother and me to take up this sport because he felt it would teach us discipline and keep us in good shape as well.

My first coach was a drill sergeant named Rick Meola. He and Tom Sebasty, an international "A" referee, ran a small judo club called Judo Tech, in New Jersey. My brother and I, along with 10 other friends from our neighbourhood, trained regularly under these two instructors for about three years.

When I was 11 years old, Mr. Meola passed away. I soon moved on to the Cranford Judo and Karate Center, a well known martial arts school run by Yoshisada Yonezuka. I trained there until I was 19 years old. These were the formative years for my judo. Mr. Yonezuka influenced me a lot.

Allen Coage, a student of Mr. Yonezuka, was an early hero of mine. In fact, even today, I would consider him to be one of the great influences in my life. His favourite techniques were *tai-otoshi* and *ouchi-gari*. These were the techniques he used in winning his Olympic bronze medal in the 1976 Montreal Games. Not surprisingly, they turned out to become my favourite techniques as well.

It was Coage who encouraged me to train in Japan. My first trip there was when I was 17 years old. I sold my car, a Chevy Nova, for $700. This, plus some savings and a little bit of help from my parents, bought me a ticket to Japan with some cash to spare. My parents were very supportive of my plans to train in Japan, but only because I had lied to them about the trip. I told them that I had a well laid-out plan and that I would be taken care of in Japan. In actuality, nothing had been planned. I had no place to stay and had no working knowledge of the language or culture of that country. I had only one contact in all of Japan, and even that was somewhat uncertain. But, in the true spirit of judo, I set off to this strange, mysterious land—Japan—the home of our beloved sport.

Although I had no guide, I managed to find my way to the Kodokan. The training there was quite interesting and I enjoyed it. There were lots of international players living and training there.There were also quite a few older *judokas* and many *senseis*. It was a good introduction to Japanese judo. The training sessions there were not quite as intense as at the university clubs but it was hard enough for a fresh-faced 17-year old warrior like myself. It was at the Kodokan that I learnt a very adaptable form of *kouchi-gari* from a player named Hara. I later modified and developed this technique into a version of my own.

My contact in Japan eventually showed up and got me into the Nihon University (Nichidai) judo club. What a culture shock that was for me! To say that it was much tougher there than at the Kodokan would be an understatement. To me, it seemed more like boot camp than

My moment of truth!

a) Serge Dyot (FRA) attempts a leg grab.

b) I respond with *hiza-guruma*, no less.

c) With a strong rotation, I manage to twist him over.
1985 Seoul World Championships.

judo training. We began training at 6.00 a.m. and ended at 7.30 p.m., with very little rest in between. Needless to say, the physical training was a complete shock to my system. I was worn out every day. But I was on a mission, so, I persisted and kept up with the training.

While I was there, a man named Dr. Yoshida advised me to train at three separate places: the Keishicho, Nichidai and the Kodokan. I was eager to learn as much as I could, so I took his advice. I trained at the Keishicho and the Nichidai during the day and at the Kodokan during the night. I did this for a week, and nearly died because of it! I even broke my middle finger during one of the training sessions because I was too tired to fight properly and became careless. I took a week off, wrapped up my finger so tightly that it couldn't bend, and continued training after only one week of rest. However, I realized that I had to reduce my training so I stopped going to the Kodokan and just stuck to the Keishicho and Nichidai sessions.

One thing that I noticed while I was over in Japan was that none of my big forward throws such as *tai-otoshi* and *uchimata* worked against the Japanese. The players were simply too strong and too upright. The fact that I was the smallest player at Nichidai didn't help either (all the players there were 78 kg and over). I couldn't get any *kuzushi* going and therefore all my *tokui-waza* failed. The only techniques that worked were smaller *ashiwaza*, particularly *ouchi-gari*. I had a particularly quick and sharp entry into that technique and this caught many of my training partners by surprise. In a way, *ouchi-gari* became my *tokui-waza* by default.

By 1981-82 I was regularly scoring with *ashiwaza* in competition. In 1982, I embarked on a European tournament circuit. My first ever European victory was in the 1982 Dutch Open. I had actually lost in the first round to a Russian named Parchiev. He took me down twice, for *waza-ari awasatte ippon*, with some kind of Russian-style wrestling technique. I fought my way back through the repechage system and made it into the final. As fate would have it, I had to face Parchiev again. This time around, I took the fight to him and knocked him down twice, both times with *ouchi-gari*. This gave me the confidence that I needed and I attacked him mercilessly, remembering my defeat earlier on in the day. A *hiza-guruma* feint into *ashi-barai* combination gave me a *waza-ari* score and eventually, the match. This first ever European victory reaffirmed my belief in the effectiveness and importance of *ashiwaza*.

While doing research for this book I watched videos of the various competitions that I had competed in over the years. I was actually quite surprised at the frequency and the number of *ashiwaza* I had actually used in competition. When competing, I often fought with a free mind and totally gave myself to the situation at hand. This was the best way for me to compete. I have found that my most common reaction against tough opposition was to use *ashiwaza*. I guess this was something instinctive, for I had never planned to use any specific *ashiwaza* against my opponents. It was just something that came naturally to me.

In the 1983 Moscow World Championships, I did not do very well, losing in the third round. In the 1984 Los Angeles Olympics, the same thing happened: I lost in the third round. I was beginning to feel as if I could never get past the third round in major international competitions. I actually considered retiring after the 1984 Olympics. However, I decided to give international competition one more try.

In the third round of the 1985 Seoul World Championships, I faced Serge Dyot of France. That was my moment of truth. If I had failed to get past that round, I probably would have retired right there and then. Dyot was a tough fighter and like most French players, his *kumi-kata* was really good. I gave him as good as I got, attacking relentlessly with every *ashiwaza* I had within me. My efforts paid off—I beat him and went on to win a silver medal that day.

The most satisfying *ashiwaza* I have ever done was the quick *ouchi-gari* attack that I used against Toshihiko Koga in the third round of the World

The final of the -71 kg division!

a) Here I am attacking Olympic champion, Byun-Keun Ahn (KOR), with *ouchi-gari*.

b) I watch in disbelief as Ahn, a devout Christian, offers a prayer of thanks after winning. The impatient referee just wants us to get up! 1985 Seoul World Championships.

Championships in Essen, Germany in 1987. Koga had beaten me twice before, in Japan. The first time we met was in the final of the 1986 Kano Cup competition. I didn't know anything about him at the time. Joe Marchal, a team-mate of mine who had been training at Nittaidai (Koga's university), had told me about him, but I wasn't impressed. I felt I could beat this 18-year old wonder boy.

Koga's *tokui-waza.*

Koga had me airborne with his *seoi-nage* —but no score!
1987 Essen World Championships.

However, as soon as we came to grips, I took one good look at his face and was immediately reminded of Kiyosuke Sahara, the Japanese whirlwind who demolished me in my very first Kano Cup, back in 1978. That day, Koga caught me with a clean *ippon-seoi-nage* for *ippon*. We met again in the finals of the 1987 Shoriki Cup. Again, he threw me with *ippon-seoi-nage* for *ippon*! I couldn't believe it…I just shook my head as I walked off the mat.

I knew that if I hoped to do well in the Essen World Championships later that year, I would most likely have to overcome Koga. I worked on a special brand of *sumi-gaeshi* that I had picked up from Katsuhiko Kashiwazaki while he was head instructor at The Budokwai, in London. I knew that Koga did not like fighting left-handers and that he was weak in *newaza*. *Sumi-gaeshi* was a perfect technique to use against him because it could be done from an extreme left-handed stance and because I had absolutely no fear of him on the ground. As it turned out, my two attempts at *sumi-gaeshi* failed to score against him.

My *tokui-waza.*

My technique is less dynamic, but it scored!
1987 Essen World Championships.

Halfway through the match, he dragged me to the edge of the mat and launched a *seoi-nage* variation that had me flying through the air. However, as he did not have a proper grip when he attempted the technique, I was able to twist out completely and land on my front.

Victory at last!

I win a decision over Marc Alexandre of France.
1987 Essen World Championships.

He was clearly ahead with less than a minute to go when out of the blue, I produced a very fast *ouchi-gari* that caught him totally by surprise. My attack was also done without a proper grip, but it scored! The knockdown only produced a *koka* score but it was enough to win me the match.

After beating Koga, I still had to face the capable North Korean, Chang-Su Lee, in the semi-final and the formidable Frenchman, Marc Alexandre in the final. However, I knew that the worst was over—I was heading for a world title.

History of Ashiwaza

*E*ver since the early days of judo, the four *ashiwaza* discussed in this volume have always been regarded as techniques which are fundamentally complementary to "big techniques" such as *seoi-nage* or *uchimata*. They have always been there, working wonders in breaking down defences, but few great champions—if any—regarded them as being their *tokui-waza*. In this sense, they were (and perhaps, still are) considered as being lesser techniques than the "real" sweeps of *de-ashi-barai* or *okuri-ashi-barai* (as superbly demonstrated by Nobuyuki Sato in *Ashiwaza*, published by Ippon Books).

Although *ouchi-gari* and its other related techniques have probably decided as many contests as throws that people consider "major" *ashiwaza*, they tend to do so with minor scores rather than the highly regarded *ippon*.

Even so, this is to denigrate such techniques unfairly. All four techniques covered in *Ashiwaza II* require a very acute sense of timing and precision—a quality that is the hallmark of a true judo exponent. Another interesting fact that I should point out is that all four techniques are tools that can be consistently relied upon by smaller players to topple larger opponents—thus clearly demonstrating that true judo principles are involved.

In Japan, where weight class is unimportant in *randori*, *ashiwaza* is a tool of survival. Perhaps that is why most Japanese players are so good at *ashiwaza*. Among many fine *ashiwaza* men of the 1950s and 1960s was Takeshi Koga of Japan. Koga, though primarily feared for his dynamic spinning *uchimata*, also had a very effective *ouchi-gari* which he often used in combination with his main technique.

In the 1961 Paris World Championships, where only one weight class—the Open—was contested, the relatively diminuitive Koga found himself up against the much larger American, George Harris. For the first half of their bout, Harris managed to kill all of Koga's *uchimata* attacks. Midway through the contest, Koga came in with his characteristic spinning entry into *uchimata*—except this time, it was for *ouchi-gari*!

Harris, well over six foot, used his height, experience and agility to hop backwards, confident that he could ride the attack. Suddenly and fluently, Koga changed direction and flung Harris over with *uchimata*. It was the *uchimata* that scored *ippon* but much of the credit had to go to *ouchi-gari*.

There are many examples of the same principle working the other way around. Isao Okano, in particular, had a very effective *kouchi-gari* which he did off a *morote-seoi-nage* entry. He threw one opponent after another at the 1964 Tokyo Olympics with this stunning combination; and used it again, equally effectively in winning the 1969 All-Japan (open weight) competition.

In 1982, the Kodokan released a special documentary video to commemorate judo's 100th anniversary. In the tape, Okano's All-Japan match against Yukio Maeda was used as an example to demonstrate that physical size is not decisive. Both men were fifth *dan* but remark-

The small man throws the big man.

Isao Okano scoring *waza-ari* over Yukio Maeda. 1969 All-Japan Championships.

It would be easy to dismiss this as poor technique on the part of the early European players but there was an important factor that must be taken note of. For much of the developing years, the *randori* (and even the competition) mat in Europe often consisted of the slack and uneven surface of stretched canvas over a soft base.

This militated against the kind of smooth reaping action that a traditional *ashiwaza* demands. It meant that to

Shigemoto (USA) attacks with a subtle "Japanese-style" *kosoto-gari*.

Brechot (GDR) attacks with a more powerful "European-style" *kosoto-gari*.

ably different in height and weight. In the video clip featured, Okano is seen attacking Maeda with a determined *morote-seoi-nage*. As Maeda parries, his stance breaks. Okano circles and watching for the instance Maeda's foot touches the mat—*kouchi-gari*! His leg taken from under him, the big man falls.

In the early days of our sport, Japanese-style judo prevailed and even some European players of that era fought with style and grace. However, this Japanese-influenced style of judo was often the exception rather than the rule in Europe, where *gake* techniques (which relies more on power) were more often seen than *gari* techniques (which relied more on timing).

score, it was necessary to use more of a hooking effect. *Tori* would hook *uke*'s leg in *kosoto-gari* and then using good upper body control, put his whole weight and pressure against his partner. Total collapse was only a matter of time.

The fact that all four of the techniques discussed in this volume have a long history can be seen by their presence in the original *Gokyo-no-waza*. *Hiza-guruma* is the second throw in the first set; with *ouchi-gari* being the seventh. *Kosoto-gari* opens the second set, and is followed directly by *kouchi-gari*. Interestingly, *kosoto-gake*, long considered a poorer brother of the *kosoto-gari*, is also in the *Gokyo* (it opens the third set).

In the official account from the Kodokan, the action of *kosoto-gake* is described thus: "You make your opponent lose his balance by making him stand on his heels as you face him directly. Clip as if to pull your partner up and backwards as you throw him." By contrast, *kosoto-gari* is a clean reap, with *uke* being taken straight down to the mat.

It is also significant that in *Illustrated Kodokan*, *kosoto-gake* was demonstrated by Hidekazu Nagaoka, a 10th *dan*, whose judo was strong and powerful, while *kosoto-gari* was demonstrated by Kyuzo Mifune, also a 10th *dan*, who being small and only 50 kg in weight, relied on a superb sense of timing for his judo to be effective.

In Kazuzo Kudo's *Dynamic Judo* (Japan Publishing Trading Co., 1967), the author, a ninth *dan* and pupil of Jigoro Kano, gives an interesting insight into the development of *kosoto-gake*:

On January 28, 1915, Hidekazu Nagaoka (10th *dan*) left his native village in Okayama, came to Tokyo, and first rapped on the door of the old Kodokan in Kami-niban-cho. Since childhood, he had studied with a Kito-jujutsu group in the fields of his home town, but his training there had centered around only the *uki-goshi* and the side fall techniques (*yoko-sutemi*). In practice in those days, the students would always stand together in a right position, and one would always slip his right hand under the left armpit of his opponent, as the custom of their school of combat held.

In those days, at the old Kodokan, the practice methods were very different from what Nagaoka had been accustomed to in Okayama. No one trained by slipping his hand under his opponent's armpit. Nagaoka thought about this a while, and decided that he would get nowhere doing things the way the Kodokan students were doing them. The only trouble was that since he could easily down his opponents using the old Okayama method, no one would be his partner. Troubled, Nagaoka stopped his training for a while and just sat in the corner of the training hall observing what the other students did—by

The first known demonstration of *kosoto-gari / gake* in Europe is recorded in these copper engravings of 1674 by Romeyn de Hooge.

a) A remarkably modern looking "sticky foot" style *kosoto-gari*. Notice the highly unorthodox "whizzer" grip.

b) A *kosoto-gake*. Notice the unsportsmanlike grip on the face—not to be used in the *dojo*.

In his absorbing account of early judo, *The Complete Kano Jiu-Jitsu*, Katsukuma Higashi, demonstrates some early forms of *ashiwaza*.

a) Apparently, *ashi-dori* forms of *ouchi-gari* were popular even in the early days of judo! It is remarkably similar to the modern-day Khabarelli-style *ouchi-gari*.

b) An interesting twist: this *kouchi-gari* is described as a block. By hooking your right foot to the back of your opponent's right ankle, you prevent him from withdrawing his right leg and getting into position for a left-sided attack.

c) This early form of *hiza-guruma* is surprisingly brutal. You are actually expected to "kick your opponent smartly at the outside of his left knee, and throw him quickly to his left."

the way, a very good training method in itself. One day, it came to him that as the opponent stepped forward and stepped backward, he always had to put his weight on one foot or the other at a given time. Nagaoka thought, "What if one were to hook and pull on the foot that bears that weight?"

This was the first hint of the *kosoto-gake*. He then went on to study ways to hold your hands, the places to put them, the ways to move your feet, the way to force your opponent off balance in this technique, the proper moment to apply the hook, and other features of the technique from many different angles. The result of his study was his own invention, the *kosoto-gake*.

Hiza-guruma, also, has played a tangential role in judo. It is not used as often as *sasae-tsuri-komi-ashi*, perhaps, partly because of the danger of a leg-grab counter. It is also technically more difficult because the hand movement required to unbalance the opponent is a large, circular one—more difficult to bring off against an experienced opponent. *Hiza-guruma* specialist, Akio Kaminaga showed how effective it could be when he threw Britain's Alan Petherbridge with that very technique in the 1964 Olympics. Poor Petherbridge had earlier been defeated in the first round by Anton Geesink with *hiza-guruma*'s sister technique, the *sasae-tsuri-komi-ashi*!

In the recent 1993 Hamilton World Championships, I witnessed an example of the most classical *ashiwaza* that I think I've ever seen. It was in the bronze medal match between France's up-and-coming Darcel Yandzi and The Netherlands's cagey Louis Wijdenbosch. As both players settled on their grips, Wijdenbosch came in for what looked like an *uchimata* attack. Yandzi attacked the supporting leg and spun the Dutch player over—flat on his back. The timing was perfect, the form, impeccable. This was *ashiwaza* at its best. Perhaps old style *ashiwaza* is making a comeback after all.

A Technical Introduction

I have purposely chosen to limit the number of words used in explaining the various techniques covered in this book. As the they say, a picture is worth a thousand words. My volume on *ashiwaza* contains more than 300 photographs ... so I'll let the photographs do most of the talking.

It is important to have a very systematic approach to training. I have organized the technical section of this book into four big chapters: Ouchi-Gari, Kouchi-Gari, Kosoto-Gari and Hiza-Guruma. Each chapter is further subdivided into five sections:

a) Basic *ai-yotsu* and *kenka-yotsu* versions of the technique
b) Special variations
c) Combinations into the technique
d) Combinations from the technique
e) Counters to the technique

As I am a left-handed player, I have demonstrated most of the techniques on the left-hand side. To utilize any of the techniques on the opposite side of the one shown in this book, simply exchange the word "right" for "left" in the description, and vice versa.

Judo has evolved and expanded so much that today there are literally hundreds of variations for each technique and even more combination possibilities. I have chosen to demonstrate the ones that I feel are most effective and relevant to today's judo. I have also attempted as accurately as possible to credit the variations and combinations covered, to those players who popularized such techniques.

In Japan, grips are divided into *hikite* and *tsurite*. *Hikite* means "pulling hand" and refers to the sleeve grip. *Tsurite* literally translated means "fishing hand" and refers to the lapel grip. The word "*tsuri*" is used because the lifting action done with the wrist is not unlike that of a fisherman when he pulls in a fish that he has just caught.

There are two basic stances in judo: *ai-yotsu* (same-sided grips) and *kenka-yotsu* (different-sided grips). An *ai-yotsu* situation, in my case, would refer to a left against left stance. This is because I am a left-handed fighter and my natural stance is with my left foot forward.

Difference between *gari* and *gake*

In Japan, the distinction between a *gari* technique and a *gake* technique is often not made. *Gari*, of course, means "reap" and *gake* means "hook." For some reason, the term *gari* is almost always used, even when it is obvious that a hooking action is involved. Perhaps it is simpler that way. For that very same reason, I have chosen not to use the term *gake* at all in the demonstration section of this book. However, I would like to briefly discuss some fundamentals regarding *gari* and *gake* in this chapter.

The difference between *gari* and *gake* is not simply that the former involves a reaping action and the latter involves a hooking action. In *gari* situations, it is the attacking leg that is doing most of the work whereas in *gake* situations, it is the supporting leg that does most of the work (the attacking leg hooks on while the supporting leg drives forwards).

This is an important principle that should be clearly understood. When working on a technique, it is crucial that you are aware of where to pay attention. Even in the middle of an attack, and especially in training, it is helpful to concentrate on the reaping action of the attacking leg in the *gari* and the driving action of the supporting leg in *gake*. If you do this, you will have a higher chance of success.

The importance of using your whole body in a throw

Although it would not be inaccurate to describe myself as a Japanese-trained *judoka*, I am rather cosmopolitan in my approach to competition. I have taken the basics of judo based on my training in Japan, incorporated different ideas gleaned from my experiences in Europe, and created various types of *ashiwaza* to deal with different contest situations.

Although I am partial to the upright, more rhythmical style of judo that is often associated with Japanese judo, I realize that this style is not something that can be expected in the arena

The importance of using your whole body in attacking with *ouchi-gari*.

a) Japan's Yoshiyuki Matsuoka, Olympic champion and *ouchi-gari* specialist, attacks with one of his favourite techniques.

b) His opponent manages to extricate his leg.

c) However, the force of Matsuoka's forward drive knocks him over.

of modern-day competition. I must admit, I don't like the bent over, brutish style often utilized by European players, but I have come to accept it as just another brand of judo. As such, it has legitimacy in its own ways. One thing's for sure: this style is something that every serious competitor must learn to deal with.

The importance of using your whole body in attacking with *kouchi-gari*.

a) South Korea's highly combative, Hyun Yoon, attacks the stylish Cuban fighter, Israel Hernandez with a determined *kouchi-gari*.

b) Although Yoon's attacking leg actually misses Hernandez's right leg, the forward momentum of his attack causes the Cuban to fall down. 1991 Barcelona World Championships.

In trying to adapt to the realities of competition-style judo, I adopted a method of fighting whereby I didn't have to compromise my upright stance and yet be effective in executing my favourite *ashiwaza*. The solution was to use my whole body in executing the techniques. Whenever I launch *ashiwaza* attacks I always begin from a good posture **but** completely throw myself into the technique once I've initiated the attack. That way, I could still fight with good style and yet accomplish what was needed in order to throw my opponent. The importance of using your whole body in applying *ashiwaza* cannot be overemphasized, especially in light of today's competition.

Ashi-dori

The type of leg-grabbing combination into *ashiwaza* that is so popular among Europeans is not at all popular among the Japanese. When I was an up-and-coming player, I prided myself in having stylish judo. As such, I made it a point to fight upright and not to resort to leg-grabbing tactics. In retrospect, I think this probably cost me some important matches.

Later in my career, I realized that leg-grabbing was sometimes necessary in order to make an attack effective. So, I compromised, and utilized some forms of leg-grab follow-ups to *ashiwaza*. For example, I could often be seen attacking with *ouchi-gari* leg grabs, and was even known to use *kouchi-gari* leg grabs on occasions. I didn't feel that I had "sold out" in any way since my attacks were always done from a good posture and **always** began as *ashiwaza*.

I never wanted to initiate a technique with a leg-grab. It always *ashiwaza* first and leg-grab second—not the other way around. The difference is probably academic but it was important to me as a *judoka*.

As much as I personally dislike *ashiwaza* that begin as leg grabs, I have decided to demonstrate

I attack my rival, Toshihiko Koga (JPN) with an *ouchi-gari* leg grab. 1986 Kano Cup.

some examples of such moves simply because they seem to be so effective in today's competition. The 1992 Barcelona Olympics and the 1993 Hamilton World Championships were punctuated with *ashi-dori* (leg-grab) forms of *ashiwaza*.

Kerrith Brown (GBR) attacks me with a very unorthodox leg-grab *kosoto-gari*. 1988 Seoul Olympics.

Timing

Timing is a very esoteric concept and one which I think should be discussed in detail. Very few books have even attempted to describe the proper timing for *ashiwaza* attacks.

A good opportunity for an *ouchi-gari* or a *kouchi-gari* attack is when your opponent's weight is on the back of his heels and his legs ae fairly wide apart. Alternatively, his weight can be largely on the foot that you are going to reap and is leaning to that side. Your hand action must compensate for the different direction of his lean—guiding his back onto the mat.

The opponent's body position should indicate where his weight is— you need to learn to recognize the situation instantly. He can be leaning backwards, obviously; or he can appear upright but is nevertheless pull-

Paul Sheals (GBR) launches Jukka-Pekka Metsola (FIN) with his well-timed *ouchi-gari*. Notice how all four feet are off the ground. 1987 British Open

Japan's Nakahara executes a smooth *kouchi-gari* on Poland's Majdan. Notice how Majdan is only supported on one leg—her left leg—the one that Nakahara is about to take away!

Karl-Heinz Lehmann (GDR) catches Ahmed Bou (KUW) with an opportunistic *kosoto-gari* counter which knocks both of the Kuwaiti player's feet off the ground. 1981 Maastricht World Championships.

ing backwards with his weight significantly on his heels. The fairly wide stance should immediately suggest an *ouchi-gari / kouchi-gari* opportunity.

Another *ouchi-gari / kouchi-gari* attacking opportunity is when he is bent forwards but still pulling back forcibly. The timing for this opportunity can be seen most clearly when you have seized the opponent's belt in a "Khabarelli" position and his reaction (the most natural) is to pull back to avoid a forward throw.

This is what natural timing is all about—the opponent creates the opportunity for your

Legendary champion, Anton Geesink (NED) wheels Sone (JPN) over with a nicely-timed *hiza-guruma*. Notice how Sone has his left arm extended, with elbows locked, in an effort to avoid landing on his back. This is not to be recommended!

throw by his own actions (though this may be in response to your move). The simplest method of creating this opportunity is to break your opponent's balance forward and then allow him to react by pulling backwards. And, the simplest methods are often better than an attempt to force the issue.

The opportunity for *kosoto-gari* is largely the same as for *ouchi-gari* and *kouchi-gari* except for the stance for the legs—the legs are generally closer together or the general stance of the opponent is more to one side.

The timing for *hiza-guruma* is totally different to the *ouchi-gari* family because the opponent must be leaning forward. For a fuller discussion, please refer to the introduction to the *hiza-guruma* chapter.

OUCHI-GARI

Japan's Olympic and World champion Yasuhiro Yamashita with the
ouchi-gari into *uchimata* combination that he made so much his own.

Introduction

Ouchi-gari means "major inner reap." The term "major" refers to the big reaping movement done by the attacking leg, not the impact of the technique. However, while it does not necessarily mean that *ouchi-gari* is a larger scoring technique than *kouchi-gari*, it is probably true that, in competition and randori, *ippon* is more easily achieved by the "major" inner reap.

Ouchi-gari is a very basic technique and it is usually one of the first few *ashiwaza* taught to beginners. Its big reaping action is easy to understand and learn although most beginners will usually find themselves on the receiving end of a massive *ouchi-gaeshi* if they are not careful. The most common form of *ouchi-gaeshi* is a simple *kosoto-gari*. It works well against any *ouchi-gari* that is done without full commitment.

Timing

The main opportunities for an *ouchi-gari* attack is when your opponent has his legs spread wide apart and is pulling backwards—or with his weight principally on the leg to be reaped. (For a more detailed discussion of proper timing opportunities of *ouchi-gari*, please refer to the Technical Introduction section of this book.)

Important points

Chest contact is always important in *ouchi-gari* attacks. The more air-space there is, the less effective your technique will be because there will be less impact. Remember to always use your whole body when you attack with this technique. Full commitment is necessary in order for the technique to work well.

Don't forget your hands. The term "ashiwaza" means leg / foot techniques, but never forget that your hands are vital for your foot techniques to work.

The classical way of doing *ouchi-gari* dictates that your head be placed on the same side as

Michinori Ishibashi (JPN) attacks H. Pollack (AUT). Notice the very strong thrust with the *tsurite* and the sharp pull with the *hikite*.
1975 Vienna World Championships.

your attacking leg. I prefer to do it the other way (placing my head on the opposite side of my attacking leg).

Allow me to explain why. One of my greatest fears in attacking with *ouchi-gari* was the threat of being countered. I came up with the idea of positioning my head on the opposite side

a) Traditional head placement.

b) My preference.

while training in Europe. I found myself constantly being up-ended (*ura-nage* to the right) by strong Europeans as I attacked them with my left *ouchi-gari*. Naturally, this situation had to change.

As they say, necessity is the mother of invention—I found that by placing my head on the opposite side, I could effectively avoid their right sided *ura-nage* counters. When I aim my head to my partner's left side, I am putting most of my body weight on that side. This makes it much harder for *uke* to pick me up with a right-sided *ura-nage*. You will see me using this unorthodox placement of the head in many of the demonstration photographs for *ouchi-gari*.

Basic Techniques

Ai-Yotsu Ouchi-Gari

a) In a left against left gripping situation, I aim for a very quick and very low *ouchi-gari*.

b) Upon entry, I pull downwards with my *hikite* hand. I also aim my head towards *uke*'s left shoulder. Notice my attacking leg is hooking his calf, not his ankle. This is to ensure that he doesn't escape my attacking leg.

c) I drive forwards and down he goes!

KENKA-YOTSU OUCHI-GARI

a) In a left against right gripping situation, I first hook *uke*'s calf with my attacking leg.

b) I use his right leg as a post to pull myself directly in front of him.

c) I am now in a good position to attack. (This technique actually involves a double motion. The first hooking action is merely to bring me into position. Once I am directly in front of him, I release the hook, only to attack a second time.)

d) I lunge directly into him with my attacking leg hooking his right leg. Notice that I place my head on his left shoulder.

Special Variations

OFF-THE-GRIP OUCHI-GARI

As the name suggests, this technique is done upon obtaining a grip.

a) I start off by cross-gripping *uke* (I take hold of his right lapel with my right hand).

b) I then lunge into him. This is done without securing a grip with my left hand.

c) I do a very low hook on his right leg while driving my body into his.

29

SWITCHING OUCHI-GARI

This technique involves a switch of stance, hence its name.
The entry is similar to that of the "Off-the-Grip" version.

a) I start off with my right leg forwards.

b) I hop in close to *uke*, twisting my hips in a clockwise manner. My attacking leg (left leg) is now forwards. Notice that I actually grab his right wrist as I do so.

c) I push his right hand away as I hook in low and deep.

TRAPPING OUCHI-GARI

a) I set up this throw by pulling both my *tsurite* and *hikite* hands close together while placing my right leg behind my attacking leg.

b) I then thrust upwards with my *tsurite* grip as I enter with my attacking leg.

c) My upwards thrust is changed into a downwards thrust as I lunge forwards. Notice that my attacking leg is hooking very low. *Uke* is trapped—there is nowhere to go but downwards.

BELT GRAB OUCHI-GARI

This technique is most useful against opponents who like to bend over in a low *jigotai* position.

a) I reach over to grab his belt.

b) I then come in with a very low *ouchi-gari* as I secure the belt. All this must be done in one quick, determined movement in order to be effective.

c) I drop to my knees and force him down towards his right side.

ASHI-TORI-OUCHI-GARI

b) I suddenly let go and quickly
duck under his left armpit.

a) I begin by pressing my
chin down on *uke*'s left arm.

Robert van de Walle (BEL) attacks Dennis
Stewart (GBR) with *ashi-tori-ouchi-gari*.
1985 Seoul World Championships.

This was the combination used by seasoned veteran, Robert van de Walle of Belgium, in winning his fifth and final World Championship bronze medal (1989, in Belgrade). This victory was significant in more than one way—the Belgian was 35 years old at the time, and his opponent was none other than the up-and-coming Frenchman, Stephane Traineau.

Interestingly, this technique was also used by one of my favourite players, Katsuhiko Kashiwazaki of Japan. At the 1982 Kano Cup, I had the opportunity to watch Kashiwazaki execute this stunning combination in his final match, against Kiyosuke Sahara, his main domestic rival. Kashiwazaki scored *ippon* with it, and retired from international competition in grand style.

c) I then grab behind the back of his left knee as I hook in with an *ouchi-gari*.

d) The leg-grab and *ouchi-gari* are executed simultaneously. Both his legs are off the ground. He has no chance of escaping.

KHABARELLI OUCHI-GARI

This is the technique made famous by Olympic champion, Shota Khabarelli of the former Soviet Union. It also involves a belt grab. For a detailed discussion of the Khabarelli technique, please refer to Robert van de Walle's *Pick-Ups* (Ippon Books), where it is refered to as *Obi-Tori-Ashi-Dori*.

a) I start by pulling *uke* down and towards me. My left hand is already reaching over his back.

b) I secure the belt grip.

c) I then begin to tug *uke* upwards and towards me as I hook in with my attacking leg. Notice that I also grab at *uke's* left pants with my right hand. He will instinctively react by pulling downwards and backwards.

d) I respond by taking him towards the very direc tion that he wants to go. Notice that I am pulling upwards with my right hand. Both of his legs are completely off the ground—there is no escape.

German World champion, Alexandra Schreiber, attacks
Christine Penick (USA) with a Khabarelli-style *ouchi-gari*.
1987 Essen World Championships.

(a) Schreiber attacks from a standard
Khabarelli gripping situation.

(b) Fearing the Khabarelli technique (a
pick-up of sorts), Penick pulls back.

(c) In response, the German immediately switches
into *ouchi-gari* and takes the American down.

WHIZZER OUCHI-GARI

A whizzer is a wrestling term for a special grip that traps your opponent's arm. The 1980 Soviet Olympic champion Shota Khabarelli often used this grip as an alternative to the belt grip.

a) I start off by securing the whizzer. (See opposite for an effective method of obtaining such a grip).

b) Next, I reach for *uke*'s left knee.

c) I then pull myself into him as I enter with my *ouchi-gari* attack.

d) There is no escape now. He cannot twist out to his right because of the whizzer that I have on his right arm; and he cannot twist out to his left because of the grip I have on his left knee.

HOW TO OBTAIN A WHIZZER

There are many ways to obtain a whizzer in wrestling. However, I have found that the most practical way to do so in the sport of judo is the method developed by World champion, Sergei Kosorotov of Russia.

a) I start by cross gripping *uke* with my right hand.

b) I then pull myself into him as I lock in tightly with my left hand.

c) I now have a whizzer!

Drop Knee Ouchi-Gari

Britain's multiple world champion, Karen Briggs, demonstrates her drop knee *ouchi-gari*.

a) Briggs enters deep and low with her attacking leg.

b) She continues dropping low with the attacking leg; so low, in fact, that she actually drops to her knee.

c) Next, she drives forwards with her upper body.

d) *Uke* is trapped with nowhere to go but down!

Karen Briggs attacks her opponent with a drop-knee *ouchi-gari*. Notice how she has instinctively let go of the *tsurite* grip, in preparation to grab her opponent's left leg.

Combinations into Ouchi-Gari

KOUCHI-GARI INTO OUCHI-GARI

This is a classic combination that still works well.

a) I attack *uke*'s left leg with a standard *kouchi-gari*.

b) *Uke* pulls back his left leg. His weight is now on his right leg.

c) I come in closer by bending forwards on my driving leg (right leg).

d) Like a coiled spring, I lunge forward into him and take away his right leg.

Osoto-Gari into Ouchi-Gari

a) In this extreme *ai-yotsu* situation, *uke*'s right leg is far away from my attacking leg (my left leg). I need to bring it closer to me.

b) I do a high *osoto-gari* feint.

c) This exaggerated movement makes *uke* pull back his left leg. His right leg is now in a perfect position to be taken away.

d) Which is exactly what I do.

Combinations from Ouchi-Gari

OUCHI-GARI INTO TOMOE-NAGE

This is a move I learnt from my wife, Chie.

a) I set *uke* up by attacking with a standard *ouchi-gari*.

b) He steps back to avoid the attack.

c) I then pull him forwards as I begin to to drop underneath.

d) Over he goes with a quick *yoko-tomoe-nage*.

OUCHI-GARI INTO TAI-OTOSHI

a) I attack with a standard *ouchi-gari*.

d) I then hop into him as I pull him onto me.

b) *Uke* pulls back his right leg to avoid the attack.

e) With my left leg extended, I trip him over with *tai-otoshi*.

c) I stop him from retreating completely.

OUCHI-GARI INTO KIBISU-GAESHI

One of the main ways for *uke* to escape an *ouchi-gari* is to lift his leg up high.
This technique is a good follow-up attack to use when *uke* tries this escape.

a) *Uke* lifts his leg high to avoid my *ouchi-gari*.

b) As he starts retreating, I let go of my *hikite* grip.

c) I keep driving forwards and aim for his right heel.

d) Once the heel is caught, there is no escape.

A perfect situation to use this combination.

Haggqvist of Sweden lifts his leg high to avoid my *ouchi-gari* attack. 1989 Belgrade World Championships.

OUCHI-GARI INTO UCHIMATA

One of the most effective combinations from *ouchi-gari* is an *uchimata* follow-up.
Here are two significant variations.

CONTINUOUS MOTION

World and Olympic champion Yasuhiro Yamashita of Japan executes this combination in one continuous motion.

a) Yamashita begins his *ouchi-gari* with a lunging action which allows him to hook his left leg deeply into *uke*'s right leg.

b) He begins his hop. Notice how Yamashita has begun to lift his attacking leg.

c) His attacking leg is now lifted very high, transforming the attack into an *uchimata*, while his *hikite* is pulling in hard.

DOUBLE MOTION

World champion Neil Adams demonstrates a two-step variation.

a) Adams first hooks in with *ouchi-gari*...

b) ...and quickly changes the attack into *uchimata*.

44

Counters to Ouchi-Gari

HIZA-GURUMA AGAINST OUCHI-GARI

Kosoto-gari is a very common counter to *ouchi-gari*. Every player who has tried *ouchi-gari* must know what it feels like to be on the receiving end of an *ouchi-gaeshi* like that. Here is an alternative that is equally effective, albeit less well-known.

a) My opponent hops in with a determined *ouchi-gari* attack.

b) I keep my left leg straight, even as he begins to hook in.

c) It looks like I'm countering with *kosoto-gari*. However, as the counter involves a wheeling action (as opposed to a reaping action), I feel it is more appropriate to call it a *hiza-guruma*.

d) He is wheeled over my straightened left leg.

Tai-Otoshi against Ouchi-Gari

This counter is based on a move taught to me by
legendary Olympic champion, Isao Okano of Japan.

a) My opponent comes in with
a left-sided *ouchi-gari*.

b) I anticipate this and lift my
right leg to avoid his attack.

d) As he takes a step forward with his
right leg, I begin to turn in for *tai-otoshi*.

c) I pull him towards me to keep
his momentum going forwards.

f) Over he goes!

e) I let go of my *tsurite* grip and
place it on his left forearm.

Ura-Nage against Ouchi-Gari

This counter is popular among Europeans.

a) My opponent comes in with a high *ouchi-gari* attack. Notice how I am already beginning to wrap my left arm around his back.

b) I pull him tightly into me as he hooks in.

c) I then pick him up with a knee lift action, hoisting him high into the air.

KOUCHI-GARI

Kouchi-gari specialist Toshihiko Koga shows off his favourite technique at the 1989 Belgrade World Championships.

Introduction

K*ouchi-gari* means "minor inner reap." The term "minor" refers to the small reaping action done by the attacking leg. Although the general impression is that *kouchi-gari* is a small scoring technique, a few *kouchi-gari* specialists have begun to change that perception.

Kouchi-gari is a very basic *ashiwaza* that is often taught as a complement to *ouchi-gari*. The fact that it requires *tori* to reach across diagonally with his attacking leg makes it a slightly harder technique to execute than *ouchi-gari* (where the leg being attacked is directly in front of the attacking leg). There is also a lot more precision involved in catching a person's foot with your foot than in catching someone's leg with your leg.

However, it should be pointed out that *kouchi-gari* is one of the safest techniques to attack with. It is one of those techniques that can used with abandon because it is not an easy technique to counter.

Timing

In k*ouchi-gari*, your task is to reap your opponent's foot from under him. The image of the reaping action is taken from the use of the scythe in cutting grass—an image that is most vivid in the *kouchi-gari* action; for you are, literally, trying to scythe your opponent's foot from under him.

Kouchi-gari is a very versatile *ashiwaza* technique that can be done from either an *ai-yotsu* situation or a *kenka-yotsu* situation.

In the *ai-yotsu* situation, the preferred variation is usually a form of *kouchi-gake* (with *kouchi-makikomi* being the most popular). This form of "kouchi" involves a lot of force and is not subtle at all. Yet, it does require timing. The best moment to hit with this technique is when your opponent is jerking backwards. Naturally, the best way to elicit such a reaction is to feign a big forward attack.

In the *kenka-yotsu* situation, the reaping form of "kouchi" is preferred. In order to make this technique work, you have to get your opponent to put his weight on his far leg. If not, he will simply lift that leg, and escape.

The best way to do this involves the use of your *hikite*. If you tug sharply with your *hikite*, you will find that your opponent will instinctively put his weight on his far leg. If you can catch that leg, you will throw him.

Important Points

There are two basic forms of "kouchi"—one involving body contact where there is very little air-space and one involving less body contact with more air-space. The former includes hooking techniques such as *kouchi-makikomi*. The latter is more "classical," involving a reaping action.

As with all *ashiwaza*, it is important not to neglect the action of the hands. Both the *hikite* and *tsurite* must be used in conjunction with the action of your legs.

Kouchi-gari specialist, Neil Adams of Great Britain, attacks with his famous skipping *kouchi-gari* variation. Notice the strong use of both of his arms. 1981 Debrecen European Championships.

Basic Techniques

Ai-Yotsu Kouchi-Gari

a) I do this technique using a mid-grip with my *tsurite* while maintaining a high-grip with my *hikite*.

b) I come in deeply with my attacking leg.

c) I take away *uke*'s left leg as I push inwards with my *hikite* and thrust upwards with my *tsurite* .

KENKA-YOTSU KOUCHI-GARI

For this situation, I do what I call a skipping *kouchi-gari*. Neil Adams had great success with a variation of this technique

a) In this situation, the leg I want to attack (*uke*'s left leg) is far away.

b) In order to get closer, I take a short skip towards his left leg.

c) I attack with my left leg as my right foot hits the ground. Quick action is necessary to make this attack work.

d) The hooking action is very deep and very sharp.

Special Variations

SIDEWAYS KOUCHI-GARI

a) At the beginning of this technique, I am situated to the right of *uke*.

b) I begin to take a few steps to my right.

c) This action gets him moving to his left.

d) When I am a step ahead of him (i.e., when I have moved to his right), I launch my *kouchi-gari* attack.

e) Quite often, a leg grab is necessary to complete this technique.

ARM TRAP KOUCHI-GARI

This is a technique I learned from one of my students, Mario Gonzalez of Mexico.

a) I start with a cross-grip on *uke*'s left sleeve.

d) From there, I wheel him around in a clockwise direction. This pulls his left leg into a perfect position for a *kouchi-gari* attack.

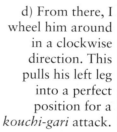

b) Next, I grab his sleeve at the elbow.

e) I clip away his leg...

f) ...and down he goes.

c) Then, I grab in tightly at his armpit.

JERKING KOUCHI-GARI

This is a technique used by Canada's Phil Takahashi.

a) I begin by pulling *uke* downwards.

b) Next, I release pressure as I jerk him forwards.

c) I quickly pull him down once more as I lunge forwards...

d) ...and clip away his left leg.

KOUCHI-MAKIKOMI

The following are two interesting variations of *kouchi-makikomi* made famous by two of my principal rivals at the 1987 Essen World Championships.

LAPEL GRIP

This is the technique favoured by Toshihiko Koga of Japan. He uses it to great effect against players who are wary of his *seoi-nage*.

a) I come in with an *ippon-seoi-nage*.

b) Instead of rotating fully, I take *uke* backwards by wrapping into him with a *makikomi* action. In Japan, this technique is called *sutemi-kouchi-gari*, indicating the commitment required.

Koga (JPN) attacks Shi (CHN) with the technique that he uses so effectively in combination with his dynamic *ippon-seoi-nage*. 1992 Barcelona Olympics.

SLEEVE GRIP

This is a technique developed by Olympic champion, Marc Alexandre of France. It was a variation of this technique that won him his match against Sven Loll (GDR) in the finals of the 1988 Seoul Olympics.

a) With both hands on *uke*'s left sleeve, I pull him towards me as I pull myself into him.

b) I then apply a *kouchi-makikomi* and take him backwards.

Marc Alexandre attacks with his brand of *kouchi-gari*. 1984 Los Angeles Olympics.

Combinations into Kouchi-Gari

Tai-Otoshi into Kouchi-Gari

This is a classic combination that still works effectively.

a) I attack uke with a standard *tai-otoshi*.

b) He steps over my extended left leg to avoid the attack.

c) I continue to pull strongly with my *hikite*. This forces him to put his weight on his left leg.

d) I clip away that leg.

UCHIMATA INTO KOUCHI-GARI

a) I pull *uke* onto me, in a determined *uchimata* attack.

b) He rides the attack, hopping off to my left.

c) All of his weight is now on his left leg.

d) I take away that leg and down he goes.

SODE-TSURI-KOMI-GOSHI INTO KOUCHI-GARI

This was a technique devised by Britain's stylish Olympic silver medalist, Ray Stevens.

a) I begin by pulling *uke* towards me.

b) I then pull his right arm over towards his left shoulder with my *hikite*. Notice that I've already begun the *kouchi-gari* action as I do this movement.

c) I continue to drive forwards as I make a big reap with my attacking leg.

Morote-Seoi-Nage into Kouchi-Gari

The brilliant Torsten Reissman of the former East Germany attacks with a combination made famous by legendary Olympic champion, Isao Okano of Japan.

a) Reissman begins with a standard *morote-seoi-nage* entry.

b) *Uke* braces against the attack and begins to pull backwards.

c) Reissman turns around and takes away his left foot just as he (*uke*) rests his weight on that foot. Notice that Reissman is taking *uke* in the very direction that he (*uke*) is pulling. This is what I call pure judo.

Combinations from Kouchi-Gari

KOUCHI-GARI INTO DE-ASHI-BARAI

This is a specialty of Germany's Olympic silver medallist Marc Meiling.

a) I come in with a standard *kouchi-gari*.

b) My reaping action causes him to lift up left leg.

c) Before he puts his leg down, I already begin my footsweep.

d) The height achieved in this technique is quite extraordinary!

Ace judo photographer David Finch catches the final sequence of Meiling's specialty: *kouchi-gari* into *de-ashi-barai*. Notice how Meiling's attack completely levels Olympic champion Robert van de Walle of Belgium. 1988 Seoul Olympics.

A perfect situation to follow-up with *kuchiki-daoshi*.

Picking up the foot.

Patrick Roux (FRA) avoids Rambier's (FRA) *kouchi-gari* by twisting out towards his right. A *kuchiki-daoshi* at that point would bring him down onto his back. 1982 Tournoi de Paris.

World champion Neil Adams (GBR) attacks with his famous *kouchi-gari* into *kuchiki-daoshi* combination. Adams uses his feet like hands, and picks up his opponent's right foot. 1979 Paris World Championships.

KOUCHI-GARI INTO KUCHIKI-DAOSHI

This technique is usually done from a *kenka-yotsu* situation.

a) I begin by taking a quick skip towards his left leg.

b) My attacking leg is used simply to block his left leg.

c) I then do a *kuchiki-daoshi*, grabbing behind his left knee.

d) I continue to drive forwards and knock him down.

KOUCHI-GARI INTO TAI-OTOSHI

This technique is best done from an *ai-yotsu* situation.

a) In this situation, *uke* is too close for me to do a *tai-otoshi*.

b) I kick away his left leg to make him take a step back.

c) Now I've created the space I need.

d) I hop into him...

e) ...extend my left leg...

f) ...and over he goes!

Counters to Kouchi-Gari

Sasae-Tsuri-Komi-Ashi against Kouchi-Gari

a) My opponent attacks me with *kouchi-gari*.

b) Without putting my leg down, I counter attack him with a *sasae-tsuri-komi-ashi*. Notice how I rotate him with my arms.

c) The movement is complete—my opponent is rotated onto his back.

Sumi-Otoshi against Kouchi-Gari

This technique is most useful against *kouchi-makikomi* attacks.

a) *Uke* comes in with a determined *kouchi-makikomi*.

b) I force him down towards his left.

c) As he has no support from his left leg, he will go down fast and hard.

I foil Toshihiko Koga's *kouchi-makikomi*
with a *sumi-otoshi* of sorts.
1989 Belgrade World Championships.

KOSOTO-GARI

Frank Wieneke (FRG) demonstrates his versatility by
attacking with *kosoto-gari* on both sides, with equal facility.
1986 Belgrade European Championships.

Introduction

K osoto-gari means "minor outer reaping." This technique is the complement to *osoto-gari*—major outer reaping. In *osoto-gari*, *tori*'s attacking leg reaches across diagonally and reaps *uke*'s far leg. In *kosoto-gari*, *tori*'s attacking leg reaps the leg that is directly in front of it. The distance that the attacking leg has to travel is significantly shorter.

The reaping action is also smaller, with the contact often involving only the foot. (In *osoto-gari*, the reaping action is considerably larger, with contact involving the whole leg). This does not mean however, that *kosoto-gari* is a smaller scoring technique for if done correctly, it can score as well as any *osoto-gari*.

Timing

Kosoto-gari in its traditional form is definitely a timing-based technique, not unlike *de-ashi-barai*. As with the case of most *ashiwaza*, the best time to strike is when your opponent has put his weight on the leg you wish to attack.

In general, the leg to be attacked is the forward leg. As such, most *kosoto-gari* techniques are seen in *kenka-yotsu* situations. If you find yourself in such a situation and threaten to attack with a big technique, more often than not, you will find your opponent putting a lot of weight on his forward leg, ready to brace against your big attack.

This is the time for a subtle *ashiwaza* such as *kosoto-gari*. If done properly, and at the right moment, you will slice his foot from right under him.

Even better still is when he is balanced on one leg. If you take that leg away, he will surely fall—a simple principle, but it works.

Important Points

I have found that very few judo books discuss the basic difference between two techniques that look alike: *kosoto-gari* and *kosoto-gake*. I think this difference is worth noting.

In *kosoto-gari*, you are keeping the top half of the opponent still with your hands, and reaping the bottom half—i.e., the opponent's leg. The general principle is that in *kosoto-gake*, you are keeping the bottom half of the opponent fixed (with the hooked leg) and moving the top half of the opponent over the pivot (with your hands). This makes the *kosoto-gari* and *kosoto-gake* two very different attacks; although they can oscillate fast between each other even in a single movement.

As I had mentioned in the technical introduction section of this book, I have refrained from using the term "kosoto-gake" in demonstration sections for the sake of simplicity.

Basic Techniques

Ai-Yotsu Kosoto-Gari

a) In this situation, I aim to attack *uke*'s forward leg (his left leg).

b) I begin by placing the sole of my right foot on the back of his left heel.

c) It looks very much like a *de-ashi-barai*, but upon careful examination, you'll notice that I am actually pulling his left leg diagonally inwards towards me not sweeping it sideways, as in *de-ashi-barai*.

Kenka-Yotsu Kosoto-Gari

For this situation, I do what I call a trailing *kosoto-gari*.

a) I begin by placing my left leg on *uke*'s right ankle.

b) Once I hook in, I do not put my foot down on the ground again.

Young Japanese superstar Ryoko Tamura attacks Britain's veteran World champion, Karen Briggs, with a trailing *kosoto-gari*. 1992 Barcelona Olympics.

c) I continue to trail him until he falls.

Special Variations

WHIZZER KOSOTO-GARI

This is a technique used effectively by the very athletic Russian World champion, Sergei Kosorotov.

a) I begin by securing a whizzer.

b) I lunge into *uke*, hooking him with my left leg as I drive my right arm into his head, securing a tight headlock.

c) I take him back, diagonally towards his right. He is completely trapped by left-handed whizzer and my right-handed headlock.

BEAR HUG KOSOTO-GARI

This is a wrestling based technique that has useful applications in judo.

a) It is best done from a *kenka-yotsu* situation.

b) I come in low under *uke*'s arms.

c) I then hug him tightly as I begin lifting him upwards.

d) I finish off the technique with a big reap with my left leg.

Naoya Ogawa (JPN) attempts a variation of the bear-hug *kosoto-gari* on Harry van Barneveld (BEL). 1991 Barcelona World Championships.

STICKY FOOT KOSOTO-GARI

This is a very popular form of *kosoto-gari*. I will demonstrate variations made famous by my compatriot, Jason Morris, the 1992 Olympic silver medalist.

a) I begin by boldly putting my left foot behind *uke*'s right ankle.

b) I take a step back, standing almost side by side with him.

c) If I feel him taking his weight off his right leg, I take him immediately backwards in a sacrificing action (almost like a *yoko-gake*).

OR

c) If I feel him putting his weight on his right leg, I pull it sideways.

d) Notice how I've spread his legs. The support is taken away from him and he falls.

STICKY FOOT KOSOTO-GARI AGAINST TAI-OTOSHI

a) *Uke* attacks me with a *tai-otoshi*.

b) I hop over his attacking leg but keep my left foot placed right behind his right heel.

c) As he tries to regain his stance, I take his right leg away.

a) Neil Adams (GBR) attacks Pink (GDR) with a *tai-otoshi.*

b) Pink counters with a timely sticky foot *kosoto-gari.*

NIDAN-KOSOTO-GARI FROM BEHIND

This is a technique often seen in competition and *randori*, yet it is almost never taught by instructors. It is actually a counter technique. Because the attack is done from behind, it is often mistaken for *tani-otoshi*. However, the strong hooking action clearly distinguishes it as *kosoto-gari*.

a) *Uke* attacks me with a forward throw such as *uchimata*.

b) I wrap my arms completely around his waist and kill his technique.

c) I then proceed to apply a *kosoto-gari*—from behind!

a) Poland's double Olympic champion, Waldemar Legien, wraps tightly around his French opponent Pascal Tayot, in the finals of the -86 kg weight division.

b) His right leg hooks in and down goes Tayot!
1992 Barcelona Olympics.

Combinations into Kosoto-Gari

KUCHIKI-DAOSHI INTO KOSOTO-GARI

I witnessed Hungary's indefatigable World and Olympic champion, Antal Kovacs, use this combination over and over again, against many of the world's best *judokas*.

a) I begin by reaching for *uke*'s left leg.

b) He straightens up and begins to retreat.

c) I pull upwards with my right hand while knocking him over with my left leg.

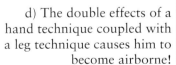

d) The double effects of a hand technique coupled with a leg technique causes him to become airborne!

Uchimata into Kosoto-Gari

This combination is commonly known as the "Twitch." It is a well-known technique that has been around for a long time, but it is still highly effective in modern day competition.

a) I do an big *uchimata* feint to get *uke* to react.

a) Roy Inman, former British coach and "Twitch" expert, executes his favourite technique on my father-in-law, Chiaki Ishii of Brazil.

b) He immediately pulls backwards. Notice how I've already begun reaching for his right leg with my left leg.

c) I finish off the technique with a big reaping action.

b) Notice the height achieved by this deceptive technique.

Ippon-Seoi-Nage into Nidan-Kosoto-Gari

Variations of this combination are used by many *ippon-seoi-nage* specialists. The principle involved is the same as that for the "Twitch." You feign a forward attack to elicit a backward pull by *uke*.

a) I come in for what seems like an *ippon-seoi-nage*. Notice, however, that my left leg is on the outside of *uke*'s right leg.

b) I continue with the *ippon-seoi-nage* grip but I bring my left leg deep behind his left leg.

c) The combination of *uke*'s reaction and my big reap takes him completely off the ground.

Toshihiko Koga (JPN) attacks Chang-Su Lee (PRK) with an *ippon-seoi-nage* into *kosoto-gari* combination. It almost looks like a *kouchi-makikomi*, but if you look carefully, you'll notice that Koga is attacking Lee's left leg from the outside.

Osoto-Gari into Nidan-Kosoto-Gari

This is one of the most commonly overlooked combinations. Yet, it is seen over and over again in top international competitions.

a) I enter with a standard *osoto-gari* attack.

Olympic champion, Rogerio Sampaio (BRA), attacks Danny Kingston (GBR) with his favourite *osoto-gari* into *kosoto-gari* combination. 1993 Hamilton World Championships.

b) It is important to maintain an upright stance in order to effect a proper *kosoto-gari* follow-up.

c) As *uke* tries to spin out to his right, I take him down with a *kosoto-gari*.

Combinations from Kosoto-Gari

Kosoto-Gari into Kuchiki-Daoshi into Nidan Kosoto-Gari

This is a three part movement. Britain's Olympic bronze medalist, Kerrith Brown, often used variations like this.

a) I begin by doing a quick *kosoto-gari* tap behind *uke*'s right heel.

b) As he pulls back I grab the back of his right knee.

c) He realizes what I'm doing and tries to twist to his left and onto his front.

d) I take away his far leg as well

Kosoto-Gari into Tai-Otoshi

A classic combination.

a) The set up for this combination is a low *kosoto-gari* tap.

c) I hop into him as I pull him forwards.

d) I extend my left leg to block his left leg...

b) *Uke* pulls backwards. This gives me the space to make my entry.

e) ...and over he goes!

Counters to Kosoto-Gari

Ouchi-Gari against Kosoto-Gari

a) My opponent attacks me with *kosoto-gari*.

b) I react by hooking around his ankle and doing a semi-circular movement with my left leg.

c) His balance is completely broken and he falls down.

UCHIMATA AGAINST KOSOTO-GARI

a) My opponent attacks me with *kosoto-gari*.

b) I make a clockwise turn and pull hard with my *hikite*.

c) I then lift with my left leg...

d) ...and away he goes!

HIZA-GURUMA

The stylish French Olympic champion, Angelo Parisi, attacks with *hiza-guruma* to both sides.

Introduction

*H*iza-guruma means "knee wheel." It operates on the same principle as *ashi-guruma* except that instead of turning away from your opponent you are actually facing him as you block his knee and rotate him over.

This throw is very similar to *sasae-tsuri-komi-ashi*, which seems to be the same technique, except that the point of contact is the shin rather than the knee. However, closer inspection tells us that there are actually quite a few significant differences.

- First, in *sasae-tsuri-komi-ashi*, there is a lifting-pulling action (hence its name). This is not the case with *hiza-guruma* where only a whirling action is required.

- Second, in *sasae-tsuri-komi-ashi*, close body contact is vital in order for the technique to work. In *hiza-guruma*, there is considerable air-space between *uke* and *tori*.

- Third, in *sasae-tsuri-komi-ashi*, the attacking foot is used as a block on which *uke* is tripped over. In *hiza-guruma*, the attacking foot forms an axis on which *uke* is pivoted into the air.

Timing

Since this is a forward technique (where you throw your opponent towards his front), it is not advisable to attempt this technique against an opponent who is pulling backwards.

The traditional timing for *hiza-guruma* is seen in the demonstration of the throw in *Nage-no-Kata*. In a left *hiza-guruma*, the opponent is standing with his right foot forward, and left foot back. You attack the trailing foot as the opponent leans forward. The reasoning behind this is that your opponent's balance is largely broken by his own action.

It is an easier *kuzushi* than trying to attack when your opponent's left foot is leading. In such a case, the break of balance would be more difficult—though it can be done, especially when you help the break of balance by creating, with a hopping action, a large, circling movement to your left.

Important Points

Of the four *ashiwaza* covered in this book, *hiza-guruma* is probably the most ignored and overlooked by many of today's *judokas*. It is often dismissed as an archaic, theoretical technique, no longer relevant in the arena of modern competition. However, a handful of *hiza-*

guruma specialists have come up with variations that are slowly changing that perception. Any player serious about high-level competition would do well to take note of modern variations of this technique, which in the hands of an expert can be highly effective weapons.

Although tradition teaches us to attack on the *hikite* side, experience tells us that attacking on the *tsurite* side is more effective. The reason is that the *tsurite* grip allows for greater control of *uke*'s body.

Two examples of "wrong sided" *hiza-guruma.*

Basic Techniques

Ai-Yotsu Hiza-Guruma

a) In this situation, I attack on the *tsurite* side.

b) I begin by pulling *uke* around in an anti-clockwise direction.

c) This will cause him to come forward with his right leg. This is the leg I want to attack.

d) Notice how straight my attacking leg is. This is very important in *hiza-guruma*. Notice also that I am looking in the direction of the throw.

KENKA-YOTSU HIZA-GURUMA

a) In this situation, I
attack on the *hikite* side.

b) I pull *uke* around in
a clockwise direction.

c) He will come forward with
his left leg. I attack this leg
with my straightened right leg.

d) He is completely wheeled over.

Special Variations

SKIPPING HIZA-GURUMA

a) I begin by shrugging off *uke*'s strong right-handed grip.

b) Next, I skip towards his left leg, almost as if I were aiming for a *kouchi-gari*.

c) I then make a sudden twist with my body.

d) This quick movement surprises him and he gets wheeled over.

REVERSE GRIP HIZA-GURUMA

This technique is a specialty of Olympic gold medalist Nazim Gousseinov of Azerbaijan. Used in conjunction with *harai-goshi*, this technique is very effective.

a) I begin by gripping *uke*'s right lapel with a reverse grip.

b) I proceed to pull his head down. This gives me strong control over his right side. It also gives *uke* the impression that I am setting him up for a big forward technique, such as *harai-goshi* or *uchimata*.

c) Instead of a big forward attack, I take a big step with my right leg.

d) As soon as my right foot hits the ground, I raise my attacking leg and block him from coming forwards.

e) Over he goes!

Nazim Gousseinov attacks co-author, Oon Oon Yeoh (MAS), with his special brand of *hiza-guruma*. 1993 Hamilton World Championships.

SUTEMI HIZA-GURUMA

Sutemi forms of *hiza-guruma* are largely used by European players.

a) This technique is best done from a *kenka-yotsu* situation.

Serguei Kosmynin (RUS) attacks Udo Quellmalz (GER) with a left-sided "sutemi" *hiza-guruma*. Notice how Kosmynin has lifted Quellmalz completely off the ground.

b) I pull *uke* into me as I arch backwards, almost as if I was doing an *ura-nage*.

c) This action completely lifts him off the ground.

d) I rotate him over my straightened leg, while he is in mid-air. This is a very dynamic technique.

Hiza-Guruma Combinations

KOUCHI-GARI INTO HIZA-GURUMA

a) I attack *uke* with a standard *kouchi-gari*.

b) This causes him to pull back his left leg. The leg I want to attack (his right leg) is now the forward leg. Notice how I'm already beginning to move towards my right.

c) I take a big step towards my right and begin lifting my attacking leg.

d) I pull *uke* forwards as I wheel him over my straightened left leg.

HIZA-GURUMA INTO OKURI-ASHI-BARAI

This is a very standard combination. Yet, it works surprisingly well.

a) I attack boldly with a *hiza-guruma*.

b) *Uke* foils the attack and I place my attacking leg back down on the ground.

c) I then take a step with my right leg towards his left foot.

d) I sweep his left ankle.

e) Both his feet are swept off the ground.

Counter to Hiza-Guruma

KUCHIKI-DAOSHI AGAINST HIZA-GURUMA

This is the most common and most effective counter against *hiza-guruma*.

a) Japan's double world champion, Nobutoshi Hikage attacks the strong East German, Torsten Oehmigen, with a determined *hiza-guruma*. Notice how Hikage utilizes his hands in executing the technique.

b) Oehmigen manages to get a good grip on Hikage's attacking leg. Hikage subsequently loses his *tsurite* grip.

c) A strong drive by the East German
takes the Japanese champion down.
1985 Seoul World Championships.

COMPETITION ASHIWAZA

Yasuhiro Yamashita demonstrates his famous *ouchi-gari* at
The Budokwai Show. Royal Albert Hall, 1986.

Competition Ashiwaza

*A*shiwaza is such an indispensable part of competition judo that one would be hard pressed to find a top-level player without any *ashiwaza* in his repertoire. While many players have chosen to regard *ashiwaza* as "smaller" techniques or as complements to larger techniques such as *seoi-nage* and *tai-otoshi*, there have been quite a handful of *ashiwaza* specialists who have made one or more *ashiwaza* their *tokui-waza*.

The great Japanese champion, Yasuhiro Yamashita, lists *ouchi-gari* as one of his favourite techniques. In the semi-final of the 1984 Los Angeles Olympics he faced Laurent del Colombo of France. Yamashita had torn a calf muscle in his second round bout against Artur Schnabel of West Germany, and was limping as he fought the very athletic French player. Del Colombo did not hesitate to attack Yamashita's injured leg and in a quick flurry of action, managed to knock him down with a sharp *osoto-gari*. The knockdown only scored *koka*, but it was a rare moment indeed. Yamashita rarely conceded any points in international matches, not even *kokas*. More importantly, as Yamashita was injured, that knockdown alone could have decided the match. In a post-competition interview, Yamashita acknowledged that for the first time ever, he thought he was going to lose a match.

However, midway through that contest, Yamashita unleased a determined *ouchi-gari* that took the Frenchman down. *Yuko* was scored. This score put Yamashita ahead, but the Japanese champion took no chances and quickly secured a *yoko-shiho-gatame* to ensure victory. Yamashita of course, went on to fight Mohamed Rashwan in the final. He won, and fulfilled his childhood dream of achieving an Olympic gold medal.

Peter Seisenbacher, Austria's double Olympic champion, won his first Olympic title in 1984, in Los Angeles. The following year, he won the world title in Seoul. He seemed to have it all—he was World and Olympic champion; yet, there was one more feat that he had yet to achieve—becoming champion of Europe. In 1986, he finally managed to achieve that, by defeating the highly combative Ben Spijkers of the Netherlands in the finals of the -86 kg division.

Brimming with confidence, and wanting to test his skills against larger opponents, Seisenbacher entered the Open division as well. Although the other competitors in that weight class were considerably bigger than he was, they weren't quite as mobile or as fast. Seisenbacher felt he had a fighting chance.

On his way to the finals, he found himself up against Britain's counter specialist, the heavyweight Elvis Gordon. Seisenbacher knew that any forward attack would prompt the Briton to attempt one of his famous dustbin throws. He took a calculated risk and entered with an *uchimata*. As expected, Gordon responded with *ura-nage*. Seisenbacher immediately switched to a sharp *kouchi-gari* which brought the big man down, proving once again that *ashiwaza* is a great weapon for the lighter fighter.

(a) Seisenbacher attacks Gordon with a powerful *uchimata*.

(b) Gordon resists the technique and begins to pull upwards, initiating an *ura-nage* counter.

(c) As Gordon takes Seisenbacher backwards, the Austrian immediately changes his attack into *kouchi-gari*...

(d) ...and takes his heavier opponent down.

One of the most notable European *kosoto-gari* specialists is the German Frank Wieneke. In the 1984 Los Angeles Olympics, the then unknown Wieneke faced Hiromitsu Takano, the highly aggressive Japanese representative in the -78 kg weight class. To qualify for the Olympics, Takano had beaten Nobutoshi Hikage, the man who had defeated Neil Adams in the Moscow World Championships, a year earlier. Takano's second-round match against Wieneke was considered to be but a formality. But, this was the Olympics and as they say, drama is the stuff of Olympics. Brimming with the confident arrogance of youth, Wieneke took the fight to Takano. In the crucial last minute of the match, with no points on the score-board for either player, Wieneke came in with his now famous one-handed *uchimata*. Takano used a clever hand-stand to avoid conceding a score but walked straight into a neat *kosoto-gari* that put Wieneke ahead. Wieneke only received a *yuko* for the knockdown but it was enough to win him the match.

This upset, of course, knocked out the man everybody considered to be the main obstacle between Neil Adams and the Olympic gold medal. Even more significantly, this victory paved the way for Wieneke himself to eventually make it into the finals and snatch the gold medal from Adams.

As I had mentioned earlier in the book, *hiza-guruma* is probably the most overlooked technique among all *ashiwaza*. *Hiza-guruma* specialists do exist although there are only a few of them. Probably the most notable recent exponent of this seldom-seen technique is Serguei Kosmynin of Russia, who has raised *hiza-guruma* to an art form.

Kosmynin's brand of *hiza-guruma* is very unorthodox and could easily be classified as *sutemi-waza* rather than *ashiwaza*. In his bronze medal match in the 1993 Hamilton World Championships, Kosmynin found himself up against the equally unorthodox Philip Laats of Belgium. Laats was ahead by a *waza-ari* and two *yukos* with only 40 seconds to go, when Kosmynin unleashed his trademark *hiza-guruma* to score *ippon*, proving that even the most unlikely of techniques can still work at the highest level of international competition.

Young upstart, Frank Wieneke, shocks the judo world at the 1984 Los Angeles Olympics.

Kosmynin attacks Udo Quellmalz (GER) with his favourite technique. Notice the commitment in the Russian's attack. 1991 Barcelona World Championships.

The incomparable Michel Nowak of France attacks his compatriot Jean-Michel Berthet with his favourite technique. Notice Nowak's clever use of his hands—his extremely strong double-lapel grip has his opponent's head completely trapped. 1982 Tournoi de Paris.

Here, we see Shota Chochosvilli of the former Soviet Union scoring *ippon* with his very powerful *ouchi-gari*. Notice the strong thrust with the *tsurite* grip. The hands are often just as important as the legs in *ashiwaza*. 1975 Lyon European Championships.

A clever escape against an unusual *kouchi-gari* attack.

a) Jong-Chol Pak (PRK) begins with just a right-handed *hikite* grip on Densign White (GBR).

b) In a quick flurry of action, he suddenly switches to a cross-grip with his left hand. White is caught totally by surprise and is forced to do a wide forward split to avoid conceding a score. 1987 Essen World Championships.

The ultimate *kouchi-gari*!

a) Japan's double World champion, Hirotaka Okada, attacks my compatriot Joey Wanag by hooking in deeply.

b) Wanag is taken over hard and fast—a very unusual and dynamic *kouchi-gari*! 1991 Barcelona World Championships.

An unusual counter to *kosoto-gari*.

a) Bertrand Damaisin (FRA) defends against Al Ciupe's (ROM) *kosoto-gari* attack by grabbing the Romanian's leg. Notice how the Frenchman has already begun to do a very high *kouchi-gari* with his right leg.

b) Ciupe hooks in deeply, determined to take the Frenchman down. Damaisin maintains his grip on the leg.

c) Damaisin counters Ciupe by doing an unusual *uchimata* from a grip on the leg! 1992 Barcelona Olympics.

Britain's multiple World champion,
Karen Briggs, attacks her rival, Cecile
Nowak of France, with an unorthodox
morote-gari / kosoto-gari hybrid.
1991 Barcelona World Championships.

Although primarily known for his *uchimata*, Japan's Olympic
champion Hidehiko Yoshida is also quite adept at *ashiwaza*. Here,
he attacks Lin of Taipei with a very upright *hiza-guruma*.
1991 Barcelona World Championships.

Luc Suplis (BEL) attacks Densign White (GBR) with
a very unusual sacrifice form of *hiza-guruma*.
1988 Seoul Olympics.